Fuzzie Wuz She

A Journey From Faith Into Transformation

Young Readers Edition

ISBN: 978-1-929921-28-7 (Paperback)

Illustrated by Jerry Thompson

Cover and interior design by Thomas Taylor

Published by

VICTORY
PUBLISHERS

www.Victory-Publishers.com

Fuzzie Wuz She

A Journey From Faith Into Transformation

Young Readers Edition

Brenda Peretin

Illustrated by Jerry Thompson

Dedication

This book is dedicated to all of God's Children.

Deuteronomy commands us to Love the LORD our God with all of our heart and soul and strength and to keep the words the Lord commanded; to let them remain within our hearts and to teach our children, and children's children diligently, whenever lying down or rising up.

May these words be shared with one and all, and may they be written upon the doors of the hearts of young and old alike. Most importantly, may they be received and believed to the Glory of Our Lord God Almighty!

> *But ask the animals, and they will teach you, or the birds in the sky, and they will tell you; or speak to the earth, and it will teach you, or let the fish in the sea inform you. Which of all these does not know that the hand of the LORD has done this? In his hand is the life of every creature and the breath of all mankind.*
>
> Job 12:7-10

Some time ago, there lived a caterpillar named Fuzzie. She had a soft furry coat and crawled about the countryside ever so slowly.

Throughout her journey, Fuzzie met friends who wanted her to change. She was not sad or discouraged by the words they would exchange.

Micah 6:8

Fuzzie tromped about with joy and song. She was happy, for God's love was so strong. She wanted to share His love, as she traveled along. For she knew, it was God alone, to whom she belonged.

Nehemiah 8:10, Psalm 24:1, John 14:21, Psalm 95:1, Psalm 98:4-6

One day, Fuzzie met Mr. Grasshopper.

She called him "Mr. G."

"Hello Fuzzie," Mr. Grasshopper, said. "Why not hop?
You'd be further ahead. You really shouldn't have to
crawl, for you'll get no place fast at all!"

Psalm 27:14, I Corinthians 13:12

"You'll always, it'll seem, be running late. Wherever you go, you'll have to wait. Then sure enough, they'll close the gate. So then, Fuzzie, what will be your fate?"

John 10:7, Matthew 7:13-14, John 14:6

Fuzzie smiled, "Mr. G., don't you see? I'm happy the way God has made me."

"Well," said G, "if that's how you want to be. But it makes no sense at all to me."

"Thank you for caring about me, Mr. G, but I'll do quite well, just wait and see. I know that God has a plan for me. He promises it in Deuteronomy."

Deuteronomy 28:1-2

"Remember too, that I have the key, and His gate is always open to me; as it is to all who believe and receive, dear G. For faith unlocks His gate, you see."

Colossians 1:14, Romans 5:1, Ephesians 2:8

"If I should turn onto the wrong way or get off the path and simply stray, I hear Him call or gently say, 'Hey.' Then I know I must stop and obey."

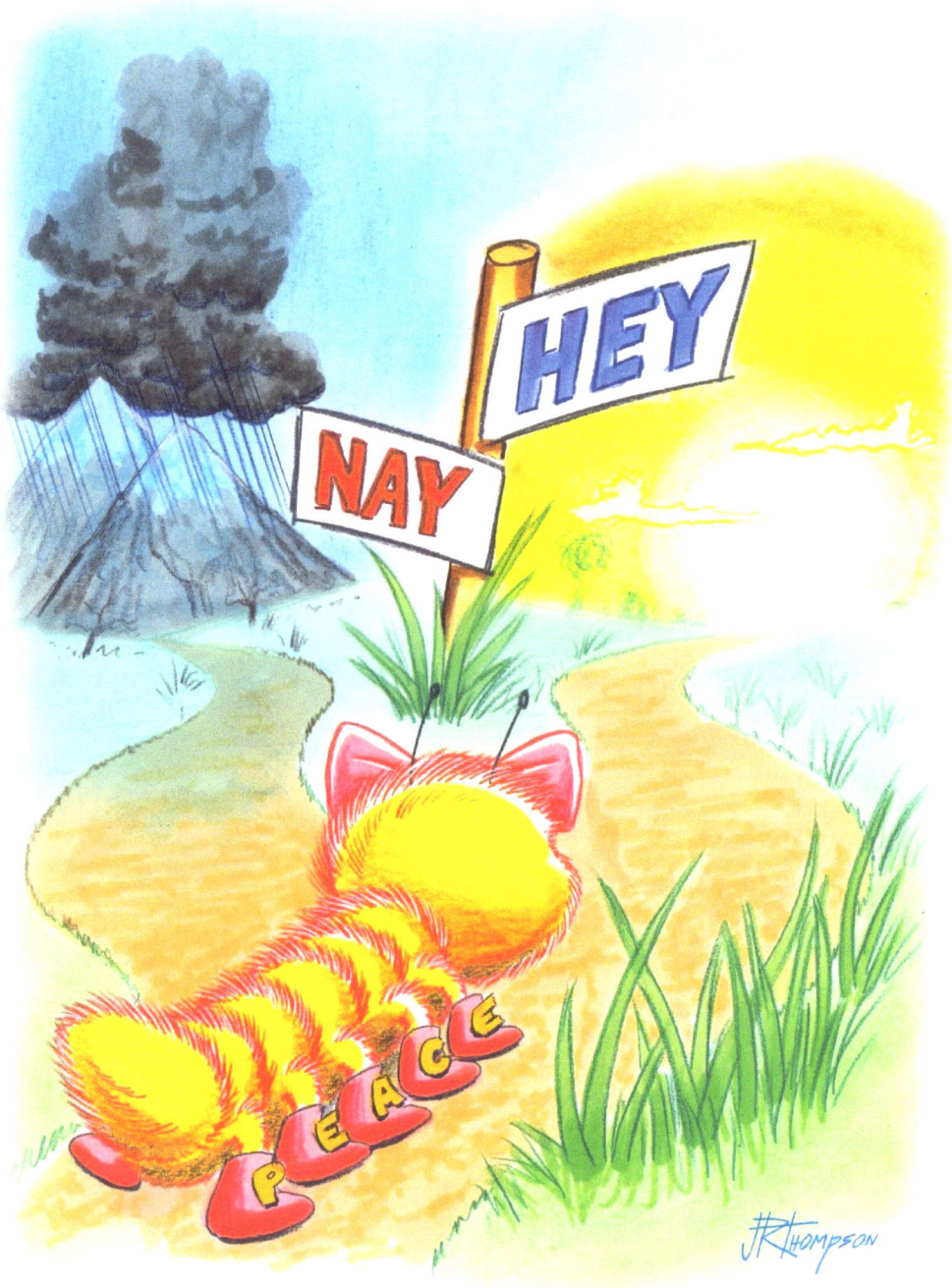

Samuel 15:22, II Corinthians 10:6, I John 2:5, Psalm 119:105

Later, Fuzzie met Mrs. Chameleon. She was ever so close to her friend's pavilion, near a flower of the color vermillion.

Psalm 27:5, Psalm 90:1-2

"Oh, hello Fuzzy," said Mrs. C.

"You've changed colors again," noticed Fuzzie. "First you were green and then brown."

"Well that's so I can't be found," chided C.

Psalm 51:10, Ezekiel 11:19-20, Ezekiel 36:26-27

"You should do the same, Fuzzie. Be like me. You'd guard yourself from untold injury," said C.

"But, I am what God has made me, dear C. And I know He will surely sustain me," replied Fuzzie.

Psalm 55:22, Psalm 86:11

12

"When I pass through a dangerous field, I know it's with His grace that I'm sealed. He is my Rock, my Strength, my Shield. And it's to Him alone that I shall yield."

II Samuel 22:3-4, Psalm 36:9, Isaiah 44:3, Proverbs 14:27, Revelation 21:6

"I put God's armor on each day, that's how I was taught to pray. He will lead and guide me on. He says this in the Book of John."

Ephesians 6:11, Micah 6:8, Hebrews 4:12

"He will guide my steps at night, because He is the Eternal Light. When I get weary, I reach for His hand and He leads me to His promised land."

Psalm 32:8, Hebrews 13:5, John 8:12, Psalm 119:130, Psalm 145:16,
Isaiah 41:10, Isaiah 49:16, Revelation 21:23

"In the 'Day of Trouble,' I'll be concealed, protected by love, and covered with shield. He will keep me in His Hiding Place. There I'll praise Him and seek His Face."

Jeremiah 30:7, Isaiah 26:20, Psalm 32:7, Psalm 46:1, Psalm 91:1-2, Psalm 91:9

The next day Fuzzie met with Mrs. Bee. "Hello Fuzzie," said Bea. "Shall we have tea today at three?"

"Most assuredly!" said Fuzzie. "There's always enough for you and for me."

Deuteronomy 16:6, Matthew 27:46, Isaiah 59:2, Revelation 13:8, Acts 4:12, Isaiah 53:4-6, 10-11 Romans 6:23

So Fuzzie shared honey and cakes by the tree, as she and Bea sipped their tea at three.

"How kind of you to share with me," said Bea.

Galatians 5:22-23, Luke 6:38, Psalm 112:9, Proverbs 19:17

"But when you share, then there's no doubt. It means to me, that soon you'll run out!"

"No Bea," interrupted Fuzzie. "Just wait and you'll see. For, more than enough is daily given to me."

Philippians 4:19, Ephesians 3:20, Romans 5:15, II Corinthians 9:8, 11

Fuzzie grew weary and decided to rest. She felt no fear because of whose hand she caressed. It was the nail-scarred hand of her friend so dear, Who was always there...always near.

John 16:13, Hebrews 13:5, Luke 11:13, Psalm 22:15-16 Proverbs 3:24, 26

Fuzzie drifted into a very deep sleep. After spinning her silky cocoon, she began to wait in faith for the Lord to create her fate.

Enveloped and wrapped in a beautiful cocoon, Fuzzie rested in the light of a full moon. The day time too, she slept so very long that many of her friends asked, "Where has she gone?"

John 17:17, Ephesians 2:10, Colossians 1:10, Psalm 36:9

Sometime later, Fuzzie awakened with a cry.

"Oh! I've been changed and lifted on high."

"See," she cried and gave a loud sigh. "He's made me into His butterfly!"

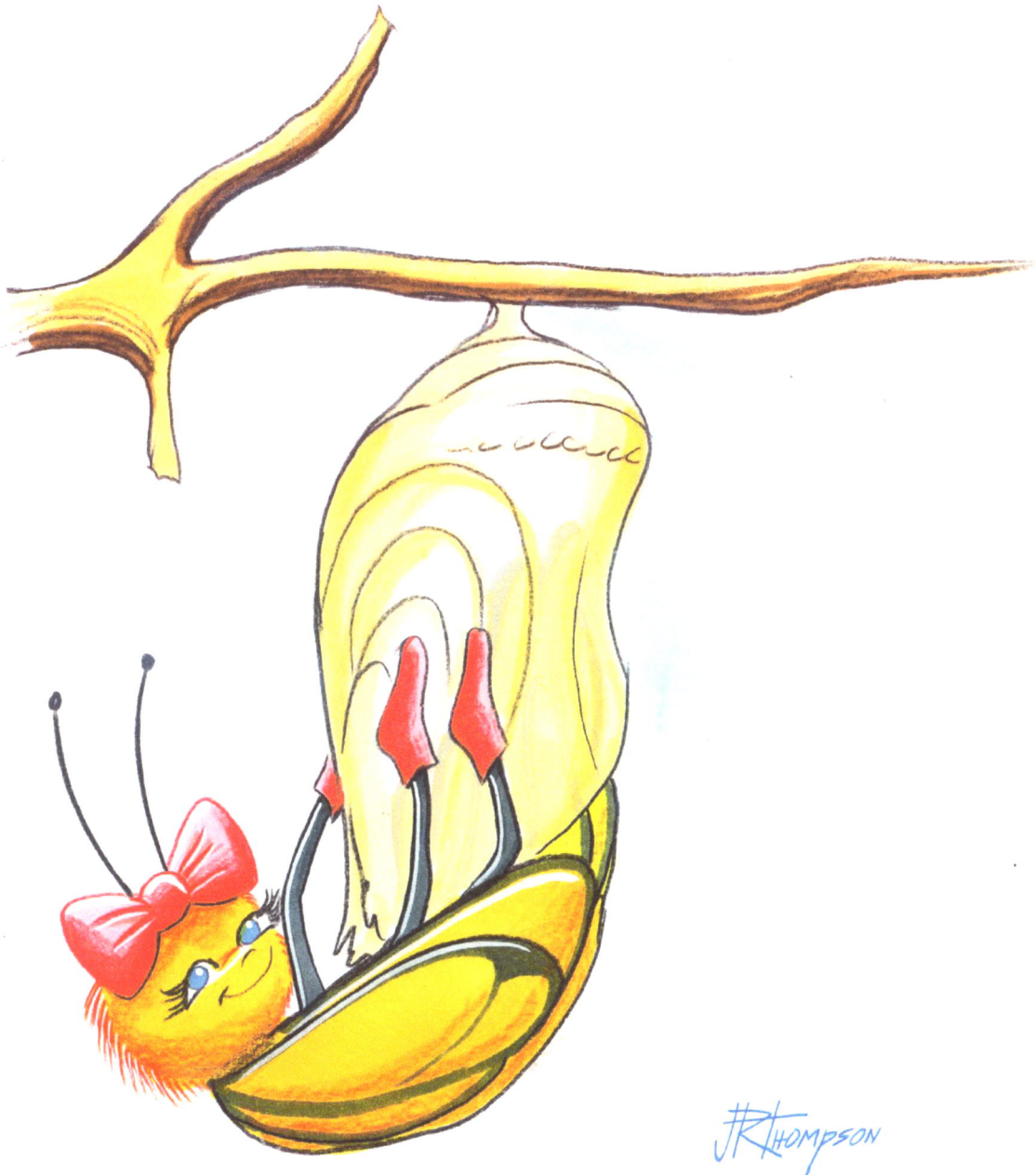

2 Samuel 22:49-50, Psalm 3:5

"Our God has changed me and made me new, as only He alone can do! And He will do the same for you if you desire to be born anew too."

John 3:5

We must Ask and Seek and Knock, for then we'll know He is "The Rock." Faith, Hope and Love are His Grace. And He desires that we seek His Face.

Psalm 27:8, Psalm 100:4, Psalm 67:5-6, Malachi 4:2, Matthew 7:7-8, I Corinthians 2:14

So all the "Good News" Fuzzie shares, because there are many for whom she cares. She desires that all would know how much the LORD loves them so.

Jeremiah 31:3, Psalm 79:13

Throughout her days, with songs of praise, Fuzzie desires to share the Lord's ways. She too might share the story of her change from glory to glory.

Mark 9:2-3, Psalm 16:11, II Corinthians 3:18

So if you should see or hear her too, then listen carefully of what to do. For she may come and ask of you, "Do you want this to be your story too?"

Well then just say, "Yes I do!" Ask the Lord to create a new heart in you. He'll help you change... it's really true; then you'll be happy and Jesus will too.

Love, Fuzzie

Ezekiel 36:26-27, Luke 15:7

About the Author:

Brenda Peretin is a nurse and an avid student of the scriptures. She has completed college-level course work in the Hebrew and Greek languages, and other studies on her way to a doctorate degree in Biblical Studies. Brenda's books are born out of a love for God, His word, and for His children who love Him, as well as those who may not even know Him yet.

Be sure to get the special edition of **Fuzzie Wuz She** for parents, teachers and facilitators, which includes questions and discussion for each story page collected conveniently in the back of the book. Entertain young readers while imparting timeless, divine principles that "***Start children off on the way they should go, and even when they are old they will not turn from it***" (Proverbs 22:6).

For classroom and group discounts, contact Victory Publishers: DrT@DrTomTaylor.com.

VICTORY
PUBLISHERS

www.Victory-Publishers.com